I Know Someone with a
Hearing Impairment

Vic Parker

Heinemann Library
Chicago, Illinois

KH

www.heinemannraintree.com
Visit our website to find out more information about Heinemann-Raintree books.

To order:

☎ Phone 888-454-2279

⌨ Visit www.heinemannraintree.com to browse our catalog and order online.

Edited by Rebecca Rissman, Dan Nunn, and Catherine Veitch
Designed by Steve Mead and Joanna Hinton Malivoire
Picture research by Tracy Cummins
Originated by Capstone Global Library
Printed in the United States of America by Worzalla Publishing

14 13 12 11 10
10 9 8 7 6 5 4 3 2 1

Library of Congress Cataloging-in-Publication Data
Parker, Victoria.
  I know someone with a hearing impairment / Vic Parker.
      p. cm.—(Understanding health issues)
  Includes bibliographical references and index.
  ISBN 978-1-4329-4560-2 (hc)
  ISBN 978-1-4329-4576-3 (pb)
  1. Hearing disorders—Juvenile literature. I. Title.
  RF291.37.P37 2011
  617.8—dc22   2010026421

Acknowledgments
We would like to thank the following for permission to reproduce photographs: Corbis pp. **8** (© Randy Faris), **9** (© ER productions Ltd/Blend Images), **24** (© Vicky Alhadeff/Lebrecht Music & Arts), **27** (© Mark Edward Atkinson/Blend Images); Getty Images pp. **11** (David Sacks), **14** (Patryce Bak), **19** (Huntstock), **23** (UpperCut Images), **25** (NBAE/David Liam Kyle); istockphoto pp. **5** (© Zhang Bo), **12** (© Darko Novakovic), **18** (© pierredesvarre); Photo Researchers, Inc. pp. **13** (AJPhoto), **21** (APHP-PSL-GARO / PHANIE), **22** (Penny Tweedie); Photolibrary p. **20** (Chapman Wiedelphoto); Shutterstock pp. **4** (© Patricia Hofmeester), **10** (© juan carlos tinjaca), **15** (© MaszaS), **16** (©Paul Matthew Photography); ZUMA Press p. **17** (Monterey Herald).

Cover photograph of Lu Zhiyan at Kuangyuan Hearing and Speaking Convalescence Center, Zhengzhou reproduced with permission of Zuma Press (Zhu Xiang/Xinhua).

We would like to thank Ashley Wolinski and Matthew Siegel for their invaluable help in the preparation of this book.

Every effort has been made to contact copyright holders of any material reproduced in this book. Any omissions will be rectified in subsequent printings if notice is given to the publisher.

All the Internet addresses (URLs) given in this book were valid at the time of going to press. However, due to the dynamic nature of the Internet, some addresses may have changed, or sites may have changed or ceased to exist since publication. While the author and publisher regret any inconvenience this may cause readers, no responsibility for any such changes can be accepted by either the author or the publisher.

10/17/11

Contents

Some words are printed in bold, **like this**. You can
find out what they mean in the glossary.

Do You Know Someone with a Hearing Impairment?

We use our ears and **brains** to hear sound and make sense of it. You may have a friend with a hearing **impairment.** This means the friend hears differently or not as well as other people.

You cannot see sound, but you can feel it if you speak against a balloon.

Some people with hearing impairments can speak as clearly as most people.

Often, you cannot see that people have hearing impairments. However, you may be able to tell by the way they talk. People who have never heard sound often do not say words as others do.

5

What Is a Hearing Impairment?

Our ears are made up of three main parts: the outside part of your ear catches sound, the middle part makes sound louder, and the inside part sends messages to the **brain**. The brain makes sense of the sound.

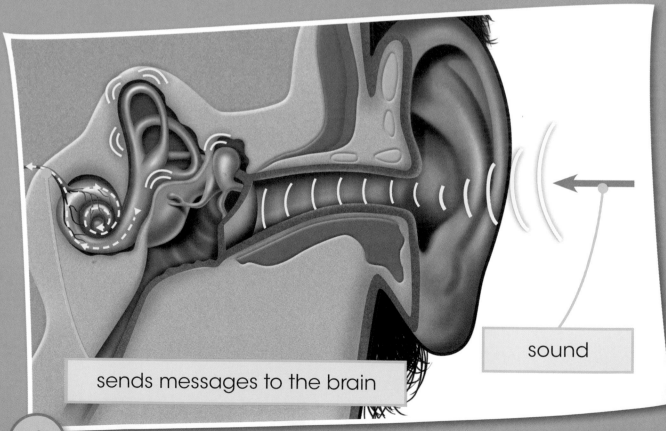

sends messages to the brain

sound

If there is a problem with any part of the ear, or with the part of the brain that makes sense of hearing, a hearing **impairment** happens.

Hearing impairments can be different for different people:
- Some people can hear some sounds, but not others.
- Some people cannot hear any sounds at all. They are said to be **deaf**.
- It can affect one ear or both.
- If it affects both ears, one ear may be worse than the other.

Blocked Ears

Sometimes a hearing **impairment** happens because sound cannot travel properly into the outside or middle of the ear. This might be because the ear is blocked.

Illnesses and infections can block the outside or the middle of the ear.

This type of hearing loss can often be made better by taking medicines such as ear drops to clear up the **infection**, or by having an **operation**.

If you have to go into the hospital for an operation, you will be well cared for.

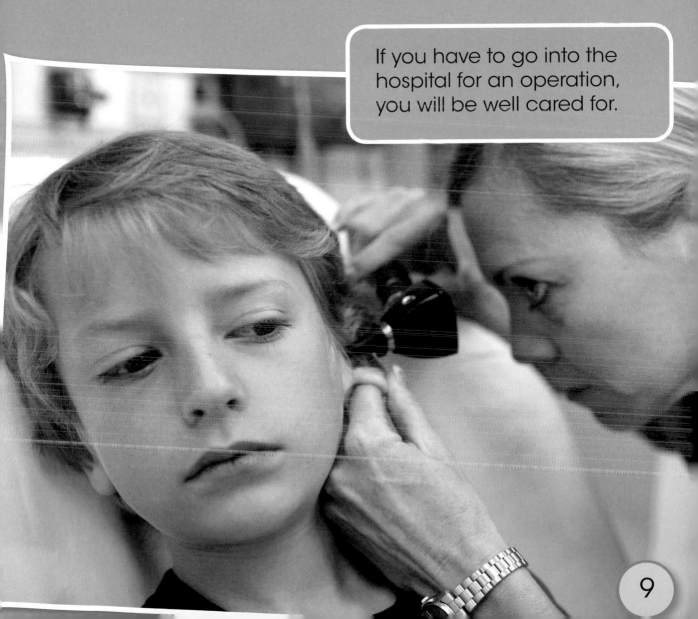

Damaged Ears

Some types of hearing damage can run in families.

Sometimes people lose their hearing because their ear, or the part of the **brain** connected with hearing, is damaged. This means that they cannot hear sound clearly or make sense of it.

This type of hearing loss does not go away. People with damaged hearing can learn to communicate by developing certain skills using special equipment.

Some hearing-impaired people can dance to music by feeling the movements made by **sound waves**.

Who Gets a Hearing Impairment?

Some people are born with hearing **impairments**. Other people can lose their hearing later in life. Hearing loss can happen at any time, to anyone. It can come on slowly or be sudden, such as after a **head injury**.

Hearing loss can happen slowly because a person has been listening to music that is too loud.

Doctors can do tests to check for a hearing impairment. The tests often involve listening for sounds through special headphones.

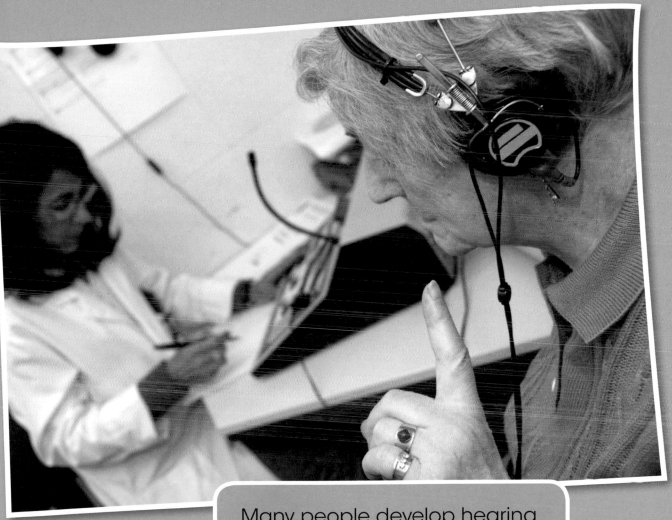

Many people develop hearing loss as they grow older.

Living with a Hearing Impairment

People with hearing **impairments** face lots of challenges each day. They may not realize when people are talking to them or not hear a telephone when it rings. They may not hear traffic or doorbells.

People with hearing impairments can have special alarm clocks that go under their pillow and shake very fast when it is time to wake up.

However, there are many ways people with hearing impairments can overcome some of the difficulties they face. People with hearing impairments can live full, happy lives.

Hearing Aids and Implants

Some people can hear better if they wear a **hearing aid**. A hearing aid fits either inside or behind the ear. Hearing aids make sounds louder and clearer.

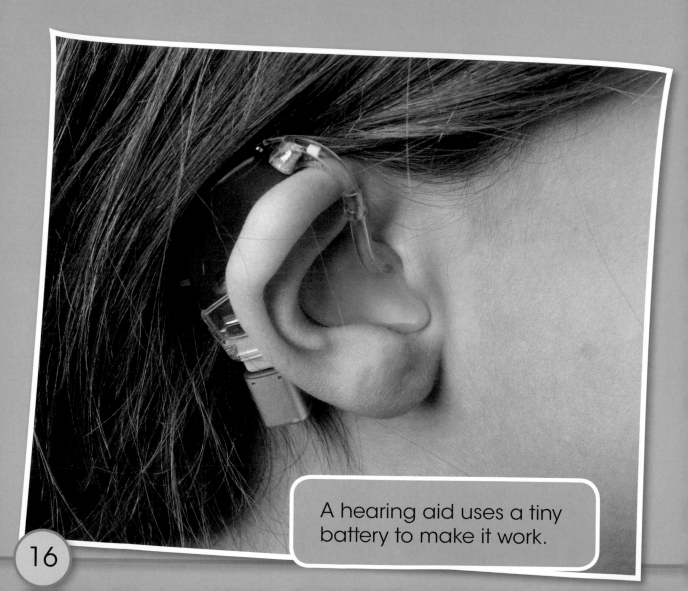

A hearing aid uses a tiny battery to make it work.

This kind of hearing aid does the job of the inner ear.

Other people use a kind of hearing aid that comes in two parts. One part sits outside the ear. The other part is placed under the skin and behind the ear. A doctor puts this in during an **operation**.

Lip Reading and Sign Language

Some people who are hearing impaired learn to lip read. This is when they watch the mouth of someone who is talking and recognize the words the person is saying from the shape of the mouth and lips.

Lip readers watch face and body movements to understand what is being said.

People who can hear can also learn sign language.

Many also learn to communicate using sign language. This is when they move their hands and face in a certain way to talk to other people. People can use sign language to build friendships and their confidence at the same time.

At School and College

Some children go to special schools for the hearing impaired, but others go to ordinary schools. A teacher can wear a special microphone that allows hearing impaired students to hear better through a **device** they wear.

A child with a hearing impairment can have a classroom assistant who knows sign language.

People with hearing impairments can do well in college.

Special computer programs can help people with hearing **impairments** at school, too. These can pick up a teacher's speech and change it into words on the screen that the student can then read.

At Home and Going Out

At home, people with hearing **impairments** can have flashing lights fitted instead of doorbells and alarms. They can have telephones that show what is being spoken. On television, speech can be shown as words on the screen.

Dogs can be trained to let a person know when they hear certain sounds, such as a baby crying.

There is no reason for hearing impaired people to be left out of any fun activity.

People with hearing impairments can enjoy going to movies, plays, concerts, and exhibitions. These places often have special performances in which words appear on a screen.

Famous People

Evelyn Glennie has been **deaf** since the age of 12. However, she is a famous musician. She performs barefoot, so she can feel the **sound waves** on the stage.

Evelyn Glennie performs in more than 100 concerts each year.

Lance Allred is just one of many successful athletes who have a hearing **impairment**.

American Lance Allred was born with almost complete hearing loss. However, he became a basketball player with the National Basketball Association's Cleveland Cavaliers.

Being a Good Friend

There are many ways you can be a good friend to someone with a hearing **impairment**, such as:

- blocking your ears with ear plugs for a while to see what a hearing impairment is like

- not speaking extra loudly or slowly to your friend, unless the friend has asked you to

- if your friend lip reads, making sure he or she can see your mouth when you talk.

We all have different bodies and personalities.

Living with a hearing impairment can be difficult at times. But there are many other ways in which we are all different. A good friend likes us just as we are.

Glossary

brain body part inside your skull that controls all other parts of your body and that helps you to think

deaf impairment that causes a loss of hearing. Someone can be totally or partially deaf.

device small piece of special equipment

head injury damage to the head caused by an accident, such as falling or being hit by something

hearing aid special device that helps a person to hear

impairment condition that stops part of your body from working correctly

infection illness caused by germs

operation type of medical treatment carried out in a hospital by a special doctor called a surgeon

sound waves sound travels through the air in invisible waves. Even though you cannot see these waves, you can sometimes feel them.

Find Out More

Books to Read

Ballard, Carol. *Exploring Sound* (*How Does Science Work?*). New York: PowerKids, 2008.

Powell, Jillian. *Jordan Has a Hearing Loss* (*Like Me, Like You*). Langhorne, Pa.: Chelsea Clubhouse, 2005.

Schaefer, Lola M. *Some Kids Are Deaf* (*Understanding Differences*). Mankato, Minn.: Capstone, 2008.

Veitch, Catherine. *Sound and Hearing* (*Sounds All Around Us*). Chicago: Heinemann Library, 2009.

Websites

http://kidshealth.org/kid/health_problems/sight/hearing_impairment.html
Visit Kids' Health to learn about hearing impairment.

www.dogsforthedeaf.org
This website is about hearing dogs.

Index